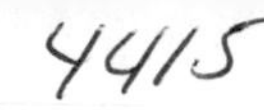

Christmas Programs for Children

compiled by

Pat Fittro

Standard
PUBLISHING
CINCINNATI, OHIO

ISBN 0-7847-1343-X

Printed in the United States of America.

Contents

Recitations and Poems 4

Presents 13

The Most Special Present 14

The Best Gift 16

Christmas Joy 18

The Most Wonderful Christmas 21

A Christmas Friend 25

God's Special Lamb 35

The True Meaning of Christmas 43

Recitations and Poems

A Welcome
Dolores Steger

The birthday is here
 Of our Savior so dear.
May our program please you
 And the Lord Jesus too. ☆

Cherub
Dolores Steger

I am a little cherub,
 And I am here to say,
Blessings, peace be with you,
 On this Christmas day. ☆

Baby Savior
Dolores Steger

Baby Savior, baby king,
 Magi, gifts are offering
To You, Savior, baby king
 For the gifts to man You bring. ☆

Christ Abides
Dolores Steger

Christ abides in a manger,
 The place where peace and
  hope start;
Christ abides in a manger,
 And always within my heart. ☆

The Christ Who's in Christmas
Dolores Steger

May your days all be merry,
 And may they be bright
With the Christ who's in
  Christmas
 As your guiding light. ☆

Why Did He Come?
Cora M. Owen

Why was Christ willing to come
  to earth,
With such a humble and lowly
  birth?
He came to us because of His
  grace.
Born so poor as He came to this
  place.

He became poor that we might
  be rich.
Laid aside glory for this world's
  niche.
Gave up His throne in Heaven
  above,
That He could show us His
  Father's love. ☆

The Birthday Cake
Dolores Steger

Blend a lot of joyfulness
With a dash of cheer;
Stir in scads of happiness,
Enough to last all year.
Mix in cups and cups of love
And then, with caring, bake
This tribute to the newborn king:
A happy birthday cake. ☆

Watching and Waiting
Dolores Steger

Watching and waiting,
Oh, Christmas draws near,
And with it the coming
Of Jesus so dear.

Watching and waiting,
I do it each year,
But praise to the Lord,
He is already here. ☆

A Baby Is Sleeping
Dolores Steger

A baby is sleeping in manger, on hay,
While shepherds and others adore Him this day;
A baby is waking, He'll rise and He'll bring
The promise to man of a Savior and king. ☆

All Is Well
Cora M. Owen

Jesus came and all is well,
Came to this old world to dwell.
To a people lost in sin,
Bringing hope and peace within.
So we choose to celebrate
Birthday of this one so great.
On this day we want to tell,
Jesus came and all is well. ☆

We Present
Cora M. Owen

We present a child to you,
Who came to earth God's will to do.
His name is Jesus, precious one.
Beloved of God, He is His Son.

We point to a manger bed,
Where the Savior laid His head.
It was there on bed of hay,
Christ was born on Christmas day. ☆

God's Christmas Tree
Donna Nevling

When it's Christmastime, there are such lovely sights.
I like most of all to look at all the lights.
But when the silver lamps against the velvet sky I see,
I think there's nothing lovelier than God's Christmas tree! ☆

Clear in Sight
Dolores Steger

Here's hoping your Christmas is merry and bright,
Beginning at dawn to the darkness of night;
So herald the birthday with joy and delight
By keeping the Lord Jesus clear in your sight. ☆

In a Stable
Dolores Steger

In a stable, silently,
The friendly beasts look on to see
A babe born for eternity;

In a stable, all around,
Angel choirs are there found,
Hear their "Alleluia" sound;

In a stable, all about,
Shepherds show they have no doubt,
"We've seen the Lord of lords," they shout;

In a stable far away,
All in adoration pray
And praise the Child on Christmas Day. ☆

On a Bright and Starry Night
Cora M. Owen

On a bright and starry night,
Shepherds on a quiet hill,
Keeping watch over their sheep,
Then their souls received a thrill.

Angels' singing filled the air.
Voices sounding oh, so sweet,
Told them to go to Bethlehem,
Infant Jesus Christ to meet.

Hurriedly, they came to town,
To a lowly manger bed,
Where they found the precious babe,
Then the joyful news they spread. ☆

A Christmas Song
Dolores Steger

Oh, sing a little Christmas song,
A little melody
Of angels and of shepherds
Who hurried there to see,
Of friendly beasts, of Mary,
Of Joseph by a stall,
Of Jesus sleeping peacefully,
Surrounded by them all;
Oh, sing a little Christmas song,
A little melody,
And praise our God who sent His Son
For all eternity. ☆

Reporting the News

Cora M. Owen

The angels first reported the
news,
Of the Messiah's birth.
Announcing it to shepherds of
old,
Telling of peace on earth.

The shepherds then reported the
news,
After a visit to
The manger bed of Jesus Christ.
The Savior they came to view.

I am reporting the news to you.
A Savior has been born.
One who brought salvation to
earth,
Long ago on Christmas morn. ☆

It's Christmas Now

Dolores Steger

I hear the angels as they sing;
What wondrous news it is they
bring,
A message of a newborn King;

I see the shepherds, wise men go
To see the babe so sweet and
low,
Then spread the word of all they
know;

I feel the hope in Him somehow,
And I, like those before me, bow
To Him; oh, joy, it's Christmas
now. ☆

The Colors of Christmas

Cora M. Owen

The color of Christmas is golden,
Like the lovely shining star
That shone on the path of the
wise men,
As they traveled from afar.

The color of Christmas is silver,
Like the tinsel on the tree
That sparkles with its decora-
tions.
It gives us pleasure to see.

The color of Christmas is scarlet
Seen in our bright Christmas
bows,
And lights shining forth from
the windows.
Oh, how they shimmer and
glow.

The color of Christmas is emerald
Just take a look at the tree.
It symbolizes eternal life
That He offers you and me.

I love all the colors of Christmas,
Red and silver, gold and green.
They make a most radiant pic-
ture,
Bringing much joy to the
scene.☆

All Is Now Quiet
Dolores Steger

All is now quiet in Bethlehem
town,
To Heaven the angels returned.
The shepherds departed to
spread the good news
Of the tidings so true they have
learned;
The Magi are gone to their
Orient homes,
Remembering those blessed
things
They saw and they heard, as
they worshiped a babe
Whom they knew as the king
of kings;
All is now quiet in Bethlehem
town,
The prophecies have proven
true;
The Savior is born and He lives,
oh, He lives
In hearts, both of me and of
you. ☆

Honor Him
Dolores Steger

Mary, sing your lullaby,
Under starry winter sky,
Hold the babe close to you
pressed,
Cradle Him in gentle rest.

Joseph, watch the baby sleep,
It's a vigil that you keep,
Guarding Him as He lies there
Safe, and seeming without a
care.

Shepherds who are listening
To the message angels' bring,
Knowing what you've seen and
heard,
Go at once and spread the word.

Wise men with the gifts you
bear,
Follow the star to the house
where
You'll present them with great
joy
To the King, a little boy.

Angels in the realms above,
Touch Him with eternal love,
'Round Him gather, never cease
To enfold Him in your peace.

Mankind, at this time, behold
The promise that was made of
old.
Then evermore through all your
days
Honor Him with all your
praise.☆

They Say
Dolores Steger

Joseph says: "One night I slept
And in my dreams an angel came
To tell me Mary's child, a son,
Is to have Jesus as His name."

Mary says: "From God I know
I soon will give birth to a son,
A child to reign eternally
As king and as God's chosen one."

Angels say: "The Christ is born,
So, shepherds, go to Bethlehem,
Find Mary, Joseph, and the babe,
And leave your sheep to honor them."

Shepherds say: "We've seen the child
And we have no more time to lose,
To spread the word He is the Lord,
The world should hear of our good news."

Herod says: "Who is this child
That all the people talk about?
Is He a king who'll pose a threat?
I'll ask the wise men to find out."

Wise men say: "We've brought our gifts
Unto the king this very day.
We won't tell Herod where He is,
We'll go home by another way."

Joseph says: "We'll rear this Child."
Mary says: "He'll grow to be
The Lord of lords, the King of kings."
And shepherds, wise men, all agree. ☆

Christmas Cards
Dolores Steger

I'm looking for a Christmas card,
One that I want to send
To someone who is dear to me,
A very special friend.

Here's one that says, "Best wishes
And may you have good cheer."
And here's one with "May Christmas
Last throughout the year."

Oh, this one says, "Fond greetings,"
And this one, "Peace on earth,"
And this one says, "We're wishing you
Much merriment and mirth."

I'm looking for a Christmas card,
And hoping one will say,
"Happy Birthday, Jesus,
On this most blessed day." ☆

Celebrate the Birth

Lillian Robbins

Christmas Eve is such an excit-
ing time,
Mixed feelings just take con-
trol.
My mom says it's always the
same
Ever since the days of old.

I want to sleep so tomorrow will
come,
But I just can't settle down.
I keep thinking about our
Christmas gifts,
Lighted trees that cover our
town.

Christmas brings light and color
to life,
And fills each heart with joy.
Children think it's just all about
toys
Brought to all the girls and
boys.

There is really more for us, you
know,
The things that always last.
Like love and peace God brings
to all.
That's real and won't just pass.

God promised to send the living
Christ
To save us for Heaven above.
It all came to be on that holy
night,
In Jesus, God's dearest love.

We're impatient to wait
for early dawn,
Our toys and gifts to receive.
But the best gift of all is freely
given.
In Jesus we must believe.

May this be a happy
Christmastime
And the joys of life be found.
Celebrate the birth of Jesus the
Christ
As the blessings of God
abound. ☆

In Humility

Lillian Robbins

There was no smooth road
Nor comfortable ride
To travel the Bethlehem way.

Travelers made their way
As best they could,
Chilled nights or heat of day.

The distance was long
As Joseph knew well,
But what could he do but go?

All the world should be taxed
Caesar Augustus decreed.
No compassion at all would he
show.

The donkey was made ready
For Mary to ride
Though her baby would be born soon.

They didn't really know
Whether midnight or morning
Or even in the heat of noon.

Of the lineage of David,
They had no choice
But to go to the Bethlehem town.

With hope in their hearts
And prayer on their lips,
Lodging must surely be found.

Many others had come;
Rooms had been taken,
Not a place they could have slept.

But a stable was near;
It was offered to them,
Just a shelter where animals were kept.

Would Joseph even dare
To take Mary his wife
To such a lowly abode?

Would pride take preeminence
Over what must be done?
Or would humility surely be showed?

They settled for the night
As best they could
To rest on a bed of straw.

Together they shared
As Jesus came to earth.
Though others never even saw.

A baby's quiet cry,
A mother's loving arms,
And Joseph who stayed near by.

The wondrous sound came
In a baby's wee voice.
In a manger He was destined to lie.

In humility He was born
In a cattle stall
To live on earth among men.

His mission in life
For all the world
Was to save us from our sin.
What a glorious gift
God sent from above,
More wondrous than we even can know.

But it was all for us
Wherever we are.
His compassionate love did He show.

Let's all thank God
For His unspeakable gift
That can never be compared.

By God's great might,
His response to sin;
His love for us He shared.

We wish for all of you a godly Christmas. ☆

Where Did It Go?
Donna Nevling

Tell me, where did it go, that
  lovely brilliant star,
That so very long ago led wise
  men from afar?
Did it just melt away and fall
  down from the sky,
Or did it shrink so small, it can't
  be seen by human eye?

Oh, no, it grew much bigger and
  it's closer to us now.
It shines right through the hearts
  of all who humbly bow,
And offer to the Savior the gift
  of their hearts,
For anywhere His throne is, His
  light He will impart! ☆

The Perfect Gift
Cora M. Owen

At Christmastime we make a
  search,
 For gifts that are just right,
For all our family and friends,
 To make their Christmas bright.

God has given a perfect Gift.
 It's meant for everyone.
He sent Him down so long ago
 His own beloved Son.

It is a gift that's always right,
 Salvation through this One.
And it will last eternally.
 God's gift can't be outdone. ☆

A Birthday Celebration
Dolores Steger

A birthday celebration
 We're planning for the day,
When so many years ago,
 God sent His Son our way.
A birthday celebration
 Is why there's all the fuss;
A birthday celebration
 For the Savior born to us. ☆

More God-Praising Time
Nell Ford Hann

Today we get cards by e-mail,
We can shop on-line from home;
And if we choose to, we can
  order
Gifts by telephone.
So many short-cut remedies,
With things . . . the high-tech
  kind,
Which makes available to me,
More God-praising time!
More time to spend in God's
  holy Word,
More time to bless His name;
To thank Him for His loving
  grace,
As His goodness I proclaim.
This high-tech age is welcomed,
When you look for good and
  true,
To seek those things that are
  above,
That it frees me up to do.
Today we get cards by e-mail,
From home we can shop on-line;
This makes available to me,
More God-praising time! ☆

PRESENTS

Anna M. Caison

A Christmas skit for primary children.

ALL: Jesus gives us presents all year round.

CHILD 1: He gave me a mommy and a daddy to show me His love. *(Unwraps a picture of parents.)*

CHILD 2: He gave me His Word so I can read about Him. *(Unwraps a Bible.)*

CHILD 3: He gave me a new family! A spiritual family to help me grow up in Him. *(Unwraps a picture of church members.)*

CHILD 4: He sends His Holy Spirit to help me when trouble comes my way. *(Unwraps a drawing of a dove with the caption: Holy Spirit.)*

CHILD 5: He called me to be His very own. And if I love and follow Him, He'll take me one day to live with Him. *(Unwraps a drawing of the kingdom of God with an inset of his picture.)*

CHILD 6: He gave us himself so we can live forever with Him. *(Unwraps the word JESUS on a large poster.)*

ALL: Thank You, Jesus, for giving us presents all year round. ☆

The Most Special Present

Bernardette Howell

Cast and Set: No scenery needed. Three teen girls and one storyteller are needed, two boys optional. Place microphone center stage with Christmas card on the floor a little beyond it. (Option of two boys walking across the stage and dropping their belongings and one boy misses picking up a Christmas card.) All onstage characters are dressed for outside. The storyteller is offstage, somewhere off to the side so he can be seen by the audience, but so he is not part of the drama on the stage.

Storyteller: This is a skit about three junior high girls and Christmas. Use your imagination and picture a brisk but sunny December day. It is the last day of school before Christmas vacation and the dismissal bell has just rung. There is a mass exit as all the students excitingly leave for Christmas vacation.

(Option: use two boys to dramatize the following scene described by the Storyteller, or let audience picture this as Storyteller continues.)

Storyteller: As two boys are heading for their buses, their paths cross and they bump into one another, dropping their books. Quickly, gathering their belongings, one boy unknowingly loses a Christmas card he had placed inside a book. As the last bus pulls away, three girls who live close by come out of the school deeply engrossed in a conversation.

(Three girls enter, quietly talking to each other until they arrive at the microphone, center stage.)

Girl 1: I'm so excited, just four more days 'til Christmas. I can hardly wait to turn on my fabulous new stereo and lie back and enjoy.

Girl 2 *(speaking to Girl 1):* You're so lucky; your parents give you everything you want.

Girl 3 *(speaking to Girl 2):* Come on, you'll have to admit you don't do so bad. I'll bet your parents will spend plenty on you for Christmas.

Girl 2 *(speaking to Girl 3):* Yeah, I think I'll get most of the things I asked for, but they won't spend $500 on a stereo for me.

Girl 3 *(speaking to Girl 1):* Do you think your parents really will spend that much money on a stereo for you?

Girl 1 *(speaking to both girls):* I'm sure they're going to. They know how badly I want it. I think I'll just die if I don't get it.

Girl 2 *(speaking to Girl 1):* You'll probably get it.

Girl 3 *(speaking to Girl 1):* Be sure to let us know if you do. I'll bring over any new CDs I get for Christmas, and we can listen to them on it.

Girl 1 *(speaking to both girls):* Great. Maybe you both can stay over one night after Christmas.

Girl 2 *(speaking to both girls):* That sounds great, but right now I think we should head home. I'm freezing.

Girl 3 *(speaking to Girl 2):* You're right, let's go. *(Speaking to Girl 1)* It's too bad we don't live in the same direction so you could walk and talk with us the rest of the way home. I'll give you a call. See ya!

Girl 2 *(speaking to Girl 1):* Bye for now.

(Girls 2 and 3 leave.)

Girl 1 *(walking in other direction, notices card on ground and picks it up, after looking at it for a moment, reads it aloud):* "Fear not: for, behold, I bring you good tidings of great joy, which shall be to all people. For unto you is born this day in the city of David, a Saviour which is Christ the Lord" (Luke 2:10, 11). *(Pauses for a moment and then hangs head, then lifts head and speaks to audience.)* I can't believe of all the talk about Christmas, not once did we mention what Christmas really means. I was the worst one, talking about how I'd just die if I didn't get my expensive new stereo. *(Smiling.)* It's not too late, I'll catch my friends and tell them we've already received the most special Christmas present, our Lord and Savior, Jesus.

(Quickly leaves the same direction as the others.) ☆

The Best Gift

Carolyn R. Scheidies

For six individuals or groups. Groups 1-3 face 4-6.

Song: "Angels, from the Realms of Glory" *(first verse only)*

1 *(Thumbing though book):* It's Christmastime.
I want a toy;
I want a book
With lots of pictures to enjoy.

Song: "Jingle Bells" *(one verse)*

2 *(Pretending to drive a play truck):* I want a truck
That goes vrr-oom
And enough presents
To fill a whole room. *(arms outstretched)*

Song: "The Twelve Days of Christmas" *(five days)*

3 *(Standing on tiptoes, indicate tall tree):* A big tall tree
Would be great
With lots of lights,
And I could stay up very late. *(Hands on hips, nod.)*

Song: "O Christmas Tree" *(one verse)*

4: These things sound nice
But don't you know *(shaking finger)*
Christmas is more than gifts
And trees that glow?

Song: "O Little Town of Bethlehem" *(verse one)*

5: Christmas is Jesus
Coming from Heaven to earth, *(motion from Heaven to earth)*
Bringing us the best gift
Just by His birth. *(hold arms as though cuddling baby)*

Song: "O Little Town of Bethlehem" *(verse two)*

6: You see, He came
To live and die for you and me *(arms out)*
And conquer death
To make us free. *(raise arms in joy)*

Song: "O Little Town of Bethlehem" *(verse three)*

4 and 5: He wants to give us more
1: Than toys and trees.
6: He offers help and hope and peace
2 and 3: For all eternity.

Song: "O Little Town of Bethlehem" *(verse four)*

1 and 2: It's OK to like presents *(Pretending to unwrap gift.)*
3 and 4: But better yet to know
5 and 6: And accept the greatest Gift *(Pointing up.)*
All: Jesus Christ who loves us so. *(Hand over heart.)*
"I have come that they may have life, and have it to the full" (John 10:10, *NIV*).

Song: "O Come, All Ye Faithful" *(verse one:1-3, verse two: 4-6, verse three and refrains: All)* ☆

Christmas Joy

A Christmas program for children

Carolyn R. Scheidies

Parts:

Preschoolers, Chorus (Primaries, Middlers, and Preteens; each group has three sections), Narrators 1 and 2—contemporary dress

Mary, Joseph, and Shepherds—biblical dress

Props: Costumes, shepherds' staffs, manger, doll, cross

Scene: Empty manger, front center stage

Scriptures are from the *New International Version* of the Bible.

Entrance: "Hark! the Herald Angels Sing" *(all come on stage singing first two verses)*

Preschoolers *(sit with parents after their recitation):*

We may be young and short and small, *(Hand on head)*
You all may be big and, oh, so tall; *(Raise hand indicating way tall)*
But we are big enough to say *(Stand proud, feet apart)*
Thank You, Jesus, for coming Christmas day. *(Fold hands and look up)*

Narrator 1: "The people walking in darkness have seen a great light; on those living in the land of the shadow of death a light has dawned" (Isaiah 9:2).

Narrator 2: "In the beginning was the Word, and the Word was with God, and the Word was God" (John 1:1).

(Primaries, step to center stage in semicircle around manger.)

1: Jesus left His home,
2: Left a wonderful heavenly throne,
3: To come to us right here on earth
All: Came as a baby with a manger birth.

Song: "Thou Didst Leave Thy Throne" *(stanza 1, "Thou didst leave thy throne . . .": Primaries on the stanza, all on refrain. After song, Primaries step back into Chorus; Mary and Joseph slowly walk up aisle and kneel on either side of manger. Discreetly add doll.)*

NARRATOR 1: "For to us a child is born, to us a son in given, and the government will be on his shoulders. And he will be called Wonderful Counselor, Mighty God, Everlasting Father, Prince of Peace. Of the increase of his government and peace there will be no end. He will reign on David's throne and over his kingdom, establishing and upholding it with justice and righteousness from that time on and forever. The zeal of the Lord Almighty will accomplish this" (Isaiah 9:6, 7).

NARRATOR 2: "While they were there, the time came for the baby to be born, and she gave birth to her firstborn, a son. She wrapped him in cloths and placed him in a manger, because there was no room for them in the inn" (Luke 2:6, 7).

(MIDDLERS step to center stage in semicircle around manger.)

1: We may be young, but we know the truth:
ALL: Jesus came for me and you.
2: Came to be both Savior and Lord,
3: Came as promised in His Word.

SONG: "Thou Didst Leave Thy Throne" *(stanza 2, "Heaven's arches rang . . .": MIDDLERS on the stanza, all on refrain. After song, MIDDLERS step back into CHORUS; SHEPHERDS make their way down aisle and kneel before the manger.)*

NARRATOR 1: "All this took place to fulfill what the Lord had said through the prophet: 'The virgin will be with child and will give birth to a son, and they will call him Immanuel'—which means, 'God with us'" (Matthew 1:22, 23).

NARRATOR 2: "'Today in the town of David a Savior has been born to you; he is Christ the Lord. This will be a sign to you: You will find a baby wrapped in cloths and lying in a manger.'

"Suddenly a great company of the heavenly host appeared with the angel, praising God and saying, 'Glory to God in the highest, and on earth peace to men on whom his favor rests.' When the angels had left them and gone into heaven, the shepherds said to one another, 'Let's go to Bethlehem and see this thing that has happened, which the Lord has told us about.'

"So they hurried off and found Mary and Joseph, and the baby, who was lying in the manger. When they had seen him, they spread the word concerning what had been told them about this child" (Luke 2:11-17).

(PRETEENS step to center stage in semicircle around manger.)

1: Jesus came to bring both hope and life,
1 AND 2: To take us to Him when we die.
SOLO: Big or small, what's important to know
ALL: Is Jesus came because He loved us so.

SONG: "Thou Didst Leave Thy Throne" *(stanza 4, "Thou Camest, O Lord . . .": PRETEENS on stanza, all on refrain. After song, PRETEENS step back into chorus; cross is highlighted behind chorus.)*

NARRATOR 1: "This is how God showed his love among us: He sent his one and only Son into the world that we might live through him. This is love: not that we loved God, but that he loved us and sent his Son as an atoning sacrifice for our sins" (1 John 4:9, 10).
NARRATOR 2: "But God demonstrates his own love for us in this: While we were still sinners, Christ died for us" (Romans 5:8).
PRETEENS: So we celebrate this day;
MIDDLERS: We make it special in every way
PRIMARIES: By laying aside our candy and toys
ALL: To worship our Savior with quiet Christmas joy.

(All kneel around manger.)

NARRATOR 1: "In him was life, and that life was the light of men" (John 1:4).
NARRATOR 2: "For the wages of sin is death, but the gift of God is eternal life in Christ Jesus our Lord" (Romans 6:23).

SONG: "Thou Didst Leave Thy Throne" *(stanza 5, "When the heavens . . .": solo on stanza, all on refrain.)*

(Optional: Director may chose to have thank yous and recognitions and/or a closing prayer by the minister or other leader)

SONG: "Hark! the Herald Angels Sing" *(last stanza; all stand and designated student invites audience to join in singing).* ☆

The Most Wonderful Christmas

Lillian Robbins

Characters: *(Some characters without speaking parts)*

Ted	Jonah's Mom
Mom (Mrs. Tetterton)	Jonah's Dad
Dad (Mr. Tetterton)	Jonah's 2 brothers and 1 sister
Dana (sister)	Aunt Christy
Granny	Christina
Pop	Jimmy
Jonah	Butch

Scene 1: Tetterton house before Christmas
Scene 2: Tetterton house on Christmas Day

Props: Centerpiece, tree, table (dining and small), chairs, stools (floor pillows or other sitting arrangements), dishes (one casserole containing food), presents

Scene 1

Mom is decorating the tree; Ted rushes in very excited.

Ted: Mom, I want to invite friends over for Christmas.
Mom: Friends for Christmas? You mean like a Christmas party?
Ted: No-o-o, not a party. I want them to come over for Christmas dinner.
Mom: But, Ted, Christmas dinner is family time. You know Granny and Pop always come here for Christmas dinner. And Aunt Christy will be here and her children, of course. Uncle Seth is going to try to make it if he can get a few days off work.
Ted: But, Mom, Jonah's family won't have much of a Christmas. They could share with us.
Mom: Why are you so taken with Jonah all of a sudden?
Ted: Well, I've been seeing him at school. He doesn't hang out with other guys. He's kind of a loner, I guess.
Mom: Is that the kind of person you want for a friend?
Ted: Why not, Mom? He needs a friend. And, Mom, I just found out his dad was laid off. His mom has been too sick to work. He has two little brothers and a sister, and now they are losing their house. They don't have money to make the payments.
Mom: That sounds bad, but Christmas is for family, Ted.

TED: How would you feel, Mom, if you knew they didn't have enough to eat on Christmas day and we will sit down to a table loaded with good food?

MOM: Well, I don't know.

TED: Think about it, Mom.

MOM: But our turkey will be just enough for our family. All of them will be here to eat.

TED: Don't we have money? Can't you just buy another turkey?

MOM: We have money. That's not the point.

TED: Then what is the point, Mom?

MOM: It's family! Ted! Can't you see that?

TED: In Sunday school we've been talking about how God gives us so many blessings. Mom, didn't God give us this great family?

MOM: Well, if you put it that way, of course! God gave us everything. I always felt like God brought your dad and me together. It's been such a wonderful relationship—and then you two children came along.

TED: Then doesn't God want us to share with people who don't have much? Look, Mom, you know what I think? I think God has just given us this opportunity to do something for somebody else. It's like He just dropped it all in my lap and said, "Now what are you going to do with it?"

MOM: Maybe we could buy a turkey and give it to them.

TED: And not share our time together, our presents and fun?

MOM: Presents? Ted, I'm not going out to buy more presents.

TED: That's OK, Mom, I'm sure I have more than enough. I'll share mine. *(With head bowed, he starts to walk away.)*

MOM: Wait, Ted. Let me look at this again. You say there are a mom, dad, and four children?

TED: That's right.

MOM: That will be six extra people. Maybe if I just buy a bigger turkey and maybe add ham to the menu—

TED: That would be great, Mom! If there is not enough food, I won't ask for seconds of anything.

MOM *(puts her arms around his shoulders):* I don't think it will come to that, Ted.

TED: I probably eat too much anyway.

MOM: Ted, I am going to need you to help me. You figure out what you can about presents. I can give you some things to wrap for them. Maybe we *can* share some of the gifts that you may have been getting. And then we'll have to figure out where all of us can sit to eat our Christmas meal; help me see how we can seat everybody.

TED *(giving MOM a hug):* Thanks, Mom. You won't be sorry.

Curtain

Scene 2

Scene opens on Christmas Day. Scene includes a decorated tree, a table, chairs, smaller table, etc. MOM and TED are setting the table.

TED: I thought Granny and Pop would be here by now.
MOM: They'll be here.

(Door opens and GRANNY and POP enter.)

GRANNY *(carrying a casserole dish):* Merry Christmas! Here's the potato casserole you wanted me to make. I hope it's good.
POP: Hi, where is everybody?
MOM: They'll be here—just running late.

(Knock on door. TED opens the door and AUNT CHRISTY, BUTCH, JIMMY, and CHRISTINA enter.)

TED: Aunt Christy! *(Gives her a hug.)* Come on in, everybody. Merry Christmas!
DANA *(enters):* Mom, I can't find my . . . I didn't know everybody was already here.
GRANNY: Come here, Sweetie, give your Granny a hug.

(Knock at door.)

TED *(opens door and JONAH'S family enters):* Hi! I was afraid you decided not to come. I'm so glad you're here now. Look, everybody, I want you to meet my friends. This is Jonah, his mom and dad and his brothers and sister. Jonah, my mom.
JONAH: Hi, Mrs. Tetterton.
MOM *(shaking hands):* Hello, Jonah. I'm glad to meet you.
TED: And my dad.
JONAH: Hi, Mr. Tetterton.
DAD *(shaking hands):* Good to meet you, Jonah.
TED *(pointing):* Dana my sister, Granny, Pop, Aunt Christy, Butch, Jimmy, Christina.

(MOM and DAD and others walk over to shake hands and welcome them. DANA begins talking to JONAH'S SISTER.)

Mom: Listen up, everybody. I know all of you are probably hungry, but we are going to open presents first. We'll just take a short time for that. Then we will eat our Christmas dinner.

Dad: That's a good idea. The first thing we should think about is the gift God gave to everyone when He gave Jesus to be born in Bethlehem. He shared His love and compassion then, and He still shares. Let's think about those things as we share together today. I'd like for us to start with a prayer to thank the Lord. Everybody, please join hands. *(Dad prays.)* God in Heaven, as we come to celebrate the birth of Jesus Your Son, we want to thank You for the greatest gift in all the world. And as we share gifts one with another, help us to see this as a way to share our love for each other. Bless each of us, we pray, in ways that will be beneficial in our lives. In Jesus' name, amen. Now gather around, everybody.

(Gifts are distributed and opened. Laughter and fun are shared. Spend as much time as the director plans.)

Mom: Hey, everyone, it's time to eat. Just find a place to sit, and we'll bring out the food. This is such a happy time. We are so glad to have all of you here. *(Speaking heavenward.)* Thank You, Lord, for this wonderful Christmas.

(She exits. The people begin to sit at various places.) ☆

Curtain

A CHRISTMAS FRIEND
Lillian Robbins

Characters:
JONATHAN
FRANK, teen
MOM Mrs. Averis
JOSEPH
MARY
INNKEEPER
FRANK'S FAMILY—Mom, Dad, Sister, Brother, Grandma, Gramps, and others (nonspeaking)
SHEPHERDS, as many as desired
AARON
SIMEON
CHOIR, soloist, or tape

Scene 1: Outside JONATHAN'S house
Scene 2: Inside JONATHAN'S house
Scene 3: In the church (at the inn)
Scene 4: In the church (at the stable)

Props: Tennis racket, tree and decorations, bench, chair, Bible, doorbell, blanket, baby, inn door with top that opens separately from bottom, manger with hay, spotlight, seat for MARY

Costumes: long robes or cloaks for Mary and Joseph, Innkeeper's appropriate apparel, Shepherds' robes and crooks

Scene 1

Outside JONATHAN'S house, JONATHAN, in a downcast mood, is sitting on a bench. He is talking to himself.

JONATHAN: It is so lonely here. I don't have anybody to talk to. . . . I wonder what Derek is doing now, who he is hanging out with.
FRANK *(enters carrying tennis racket):* Hi! I just noticed you sitting here, and—are you okay? Something wrong?

JONATHAN: No—I just miss my friends.

FRANK: Where are your friends? Have they gone off somewhere without you?

JONATHAN: They're back in Ohio. My mom and I just moved here.

FRANK: My name is Frank. I go to the high school on North Road, but I live just a couple blocks down the street from here.

JONATHAN: I'm Jonathan.

FRANK: I was on my way to the rec center—they have indoor tennis courts. Do you like to play tennis?

JONATHAN: I don't know how, but I guess it could be fun.

FRANK: I don't have to play tennis right now. Maybe we can just talk.

JONATHAN: You're going to stay and talk to me?

FRANK *(sits down):* Sure, why not? Did you have a lot of friends in Ohio?

JONATHAN: Well, you might say so.

FRANK: Tell me about them. Were they boys your age? Were there a lot of neighborhood kids to hang out with?

JONATHAN: The guys were different ages, but my best friend was Derek. He was the best friend in the world. We did things together. We could talk about stuff, and he was always there for me. If I called him to come over, he'd be there in a flash. He could make me laugh—and he knew everything! If I was stumped on homework, he could always help me.

FRANK: Derek sounds like a good friend to have.

JONATHAN: He was the best! Now I'm so lonely, and I can't call him to come over.

FRANK: Well, Christmas is coming soon. You can get excited about that.

JONATHAN: Christmas won't be any fun without Derek! We always got up early on Christmas morning. As soon as we opened our presents, he would come to my house or I'd go over to his place. We'd share our toys, make popcorn, laugh and joke, and just have a good time.

FRANK: Don't you have any friends here, Jonathan?

JONATHAN: Not really. There are guys at school—but they all hang out in groups. I just don't seem to fit in anywhere.

FRANK: How about people in the neighborhood?

JONATHAN: I don't see many. Some guys ride bikes by here, and some skate, but they never stop. *(JONATHAN heaves a sigh.)* I just don't know anyone around here.

FRANK: Do you know Jesus?

JONATHAN: Who?

FRANK: Jesus, you know—you read about Him in the Bible.

JONATHAN: I don't know about that.

FRANK: You don't know about Jesus or you don't know about the Bible?

JONATHAN: I don't really know what you're talking about.

FRANK *(looks up, speaks quietly and earnestly):* Lord, please help me reach Jonathan.

JONATHAN *(looking at Frank):* What did you say?

FRANK: I have a friend I want you to meet. He can be your friend, too. He will always be there for you. If you're sad, He finds ways to make you happy. You can call on Him anytime. And, Jonathan, this special friend has an answer for everything.

JONATHAN: He may not want to be my friend. Anyway, nobody can take the place of Derek.

FRANK: This friend will not even want to take the place of Derek. He will just be your special friend. You'll never have to move away and leave Him. He will always be your special friend, even when you grow up and go to college.

JONATHAN *(countenance brightens):* Who is this friend of yours?

FRANK: His name is Jesus.

JONATHAN: The one you asked me about?

FRANK: That's right, the one I asked you about, and I want you to meet Him right away. I have an idea.

JONATHAN: What kind of idea?

FRANK: I'm going to bring you a Bible and introduce you to Him. And this Sunday night, I'd like you to go with me to a Christmas celebration at church. You will be thrilled when you see the inn at Bethlehem, the stable where the baby lay, the—well, just wait and see. It will be great.

JONATHAN: I don't know that my mom will let me go.

FRANK: She can come, too. There will be a lot of adults there. It's for everyone. Gramps and my Grandma always go with us. Actually, they live in another town, but they love this Christmas celebration so much they always come.

JONATHAN: OK. I'll check with my mom.

FRANK: Just remember, Christmas is always a happy time when you put Jesus right smack in the middle of it. This may be the very best Christmas you ever had.

JONATHAN: What about presents? Do we have to bring presents?

FRANK: No, you just need to be there. Don't worry. You'll see. *(Frank prepares to leave.)* I'll be back and bring you a Bible. Maybe I can meet your mom then. *(Walks away.)*

JONATHAN *(goes toward FRANK):* Frank, wait up. What should I wear to this Christmas celebration you're talking about?

Frank: Just regular clothes. What you're wearing now is fine. *(Walking away.)* See you, Jonathan.
Jonathan: Yeah, see you.

Curtain

Scene 2

In Jonathan's family room, Mom is decorating the tree. Most of the decorations are already on: outlandish, colorful beads, garlands, etc. Wrapped Christmas boxes are stacked around the tree.

Jonathan *(enters):* Hey, Mom, did you see that guy who was just talking to me?
Mom *(continues decorating):* No, I didn't see anyone. I've been busy decorating this tree. Still got a lot more to do. You know we always get our tree up earlier than this, but with the moving and everything, it's really late this year.
Jonathan: I think the guy is pretty cool. His name is Frank. He goes to that high school out on North Road.
Mom: Really?
Jonathan: Yeah, he was on his way to play tennis, but he stopped to talk to me. I was surprised. Most people seem too busy to notice you, much less stop to talk.
Mom: That's nice.
Jonathan: He's kinda big. But he doesn't act all arrogant and stuff—just a regular guy.

(Mom doesn't respond.)

Jonathan *(emphatically):* Mom, are you listening to me?
Mom *(looking at him):* Oh, sure, do you want something?
Jonathan: Just to have you talk to me. I don't have anybody to talk to since we moved. Frank is the first person who has even told me his name.
Mom: Frank? Who is Frank?
Jonathan: I was just telling you—the guy who stopped by out there to talk to me.
Mom: What did he want?
Jonathan: He didn't want anything. He was just being friendly.

MOM *(starts back to the tree):* That's good.
JONATHAN *(taking her hand):* Mom, wait a minute!
MOM: Jonathan, you know I have so much to do. I've got to finish this tree, wrap two or three more boxes, fix our supper—
JONATHAN: But, Mom, I need you to listen to me. I have more to tell you —about what Frank said. Come sit down for just one minute, please.
MOM *(moving to sofa):* Oh, all right; just one minute then!
JONATHAN: See, Mom, I was telling Frank about Derek, how much I miss him . . .
MOM: I know, Jonathan, I miss my old friends, too. But it'll get better after a while.
JONATHAN: Anyway, Frank . . . *(doorbell rings).* I'll get it. *(Opens door, Frank enters.)* Hi, Frank. You came back just as you said you would.
FRANK: I live just two blocks down the street. It didn't take long.
JONATHAN: Come on in. This is my mom. We were just talking about you.
FRANK *(extending hand):* Good to meet you, Mrs. —-Ah?
MOM: Mrs. Averis. Likewise, good to meet you.
FRANK: My, what a big Christmas tree! And so colorful!
MOM: I know. People always say I have the strangest looking Christmas tree. But I like it this way. I don't care for lights, but I like color.
JONATHAN: Our tree always looks different from everybody else's.
FRANK: And so many presents! You must have a very big family or a lot of friends.
MOM *(laughing):* Actually, it's neither. I just like it to seem like a lot of presents. I wrap empty boxes and just stack them all around. I'm pretty good at pretending.
FRANK: You seem to be enjoying it.
MOM: Well . . .
JONATHAN: Mom's busy all the time, though. She almost never sits down.
FRANK: I told Jonathan I would bring him a Bible. I wanted to get it to him right away so he could read some before Sunday night.
MOM: I have a Bible around here somewhere.
FRANK: I thought Jonathan might like to have one of his own. Actually, this is the Bible I used to read and study, but I want Jonathan to have it. *(Hands it over to Jonathan)*
JONATHAN *(taking the Bible):* But, Frank, if this is your book, I don't want to take it away from you.
FRANK: Jonathan, this is not just a *book.* It's more special than any book you will ever read. And I can get another one for me.
MOM: I don't know that Jonathan will care to read it.

Frank: You might be surprised. As I was telling Jonathan, Sunday night is the time for our special Christmas celebration at church. I was hoping you and Jonathan could go with our family.

Jonathan: Frank, I haven't had a chance to talk to Mom about that yet.

Mom *(getting up):* I've got to get back to work. You two can talk on as much as you like.

Jonathan: That's the way it is—always. She never has time to talk.

Frank: Let's just sit here a minute. My time is your time, and I want to show you here in the Bible where you can read about the first Christmas.

(Mom is busy with the tree but occasionally stops to listen.)

Jonathan: It's such a big book.

Frank: True, but it's in sections so it's easy to read just the part you want to read at anytime. *(Opens Bible)* Now here is the book of Luke. See? I've written down the part I'd like you to read before Sunday. When you read this part, you'll see how an angel appeared to a woman named Mary. The angel said Mary was going to have a baby boy, and His name would be Jesus. *(Turns to Luke 2)* When you read on into this chapter, you'll read about the first Christmas.

Jonathan: That looks like a lot to read.

Frank: Not really. Just remember that God loves all of us, and that includes you, Jonathan. He loves us so much He sent His Son to earth to save us.

Jonathan: I'm not sure I'll understand all this.

Frank: If you'll just read this in the Bible, when you see the Christmas pageant, it will seem more real. And, Jonathan, if there is anything you don't understand, you and I can talk about it. *(Stands up to go)* I'd better get going now. See you, Jonathan. So long, Mrs. Averis.

Mom: Bye, Frank. See you.

(Frank leaves. Mom comes over to Jonathan, who already has started to read.)

Mom: What about this Christmas celebration you two were talking about?

Jonathan: It's at their church. Frank said we can go with his family.

Mom: How much does it cost?

Jonathan: I don't think it's something you pay for. Frank didn't say anything about money. When I asked him if we need to take presents, he said, "Just be there." Frank says it's great and I want to go.

MOM: Well, I guess if I get all my work caught up, unpack all those other boxes, find something decent to wear—

JONATHAN: Mom, just go! That's all you have to do!

Curtain

Scene 3

FRANK'S family, JONATHAN and MRS. AVERIS come and sit in front of the auditorium. Seats will be reserved. On stage are bales of hay and front of an inn with split door so top half can open separately from bottom.

JOSEPH *(enters helping MARY along):* You can sit right here, Mary. I'll put this blanket over the hay. It will be more comfortable than riding the donkey over those long, bumpy paths. *(Spreads blanket for MARY to sit on.)* I won't be long, Mary. I just have to get a place for us to sleep tonight.

(JOSEPH goes to door and knocks, no answer; knocks again with no answer; knocks again harder, and the top door opens.)

INNKEEPER: What do you want?

JOSEPH: My wife and I need a place to sleep.

INNKEEPER: The inn is full. *(Starts to close door.)*

JOSEPH: No, wait! There is my wife over there. *(Pointing)* As you can see, she is expecting a child, maybe even tonight. We must have a place.

INNKEEPER: You came to Bethlehem for the taxing as Caesar Augustus demanded?

JOSEPH: Yes, we are of the lineage of David.

INNKEEPER: Where did you come from?

JOSEPH: Nazareth of Galilee. It has been a very long journey for Mary.

INNKEEPER: I would think so. But why didn't you come earlier in the day before all the rooms were filled?

JOSEPH: We couldn't travel very fast. We had to make several stops along the way for Mary. If your wife ever had children, you know how it is.

INNKEEPER: Yes, of course. I wish there was something I could do, but I can't very well ask someone to give up his room for you.

JOSEPH: But there must be a place. I know there is a way. The Lord would not just leave us out in the cold. I just don't know right now what to do.

Mary *(calling out, her discomfort obvious):* Joseph!

Joseph: Yes, Mary, I'll be there. *(To the Innkeeper)* You see how it is. Where can I find a place for Mary to stay tonight?

Innkeeper: I know of only one place. You could go down to the stable. There is plenty of fresh hay there. You could make a bed for her in the stable. I know that's not much to offer, but at least she would have shelter and a place to lie down.

Joseph: Yes, you are right.

Innkeeper: Just lead your donkey right down that way. *(Points)* There is plenty of room for your donkey too and you can feed him some of the hay.

Joseph: Thank you. We'll go right along. *(Joseph returns to Mary and together they leave.)*

Innkeeper: I wonder if Caesar Augustus will ever know how much of a burden he has put on our people by requiring them to go back to their hometowns. If he had just arranged for the listing to be done in the towns where the people live, this poor young woman wouldn't be in this situation now in a strange city here in Bethlehem.

Curtain

Scene 4

Spotlight on the manger scene. Mary sits beside manger where the baby lies. Joseph stands nearby.

Joseph: Mary, are you all right?

Mary: Yes, Joseph. Thank you for your concern. But now I want to hold Him, my precious little boy.

(Joseph lifts the baby out of the manger and places Him in Mary's lap.)

Joseph: This is a very special little boy, Mary. We knew because the angel told us you would give birth to God's Son, but we could never be certain just how it would come to pass, especially having to travel here from Nazareth.

Mary: But we always knew God would take care of us, Joseph. I think our Son has such a beautiful name, the name the angel said to give Him, Jesus. It sounds like music when I say it—Jesus.

Joseph: I remember when the angel said to me, "Call his name Jesus"—Savior—"for he shall save his people from their sins" (Matthew 1:21).

Mary: It's the fulfillment of Isaiah's prophecy: "'They shall call his name Immanuel,' which being interpreted is, God with us" (Matthew 1:23).
Joseph: *(touches the face of the baby.)* Mary, can you imagine, God with us! What a wonderful miracle God has given to us and to all people from this day forward.
Mary: We must thank the Lord God for providing this place for Jesus to be born. I am really content and happy. We were never alone, you know. God was always with us.

(Joseph puts the baby back in the manger. Spotlight dims.)

Soloist: "O Holy Night"

(As a bright light shines in the distance, voices are heard.)

Simeon: Look, Aaron, look at that light!
Aaron: What is it? What does it mean? What should we do?
Simeon: I don't know. It's frightening!
Angel: Don't be afraid. I've come to bring you good news which will be to all people. For unto you is born this day a Savior which is Christ the Lord. You will find the baby in Bethlehem where he lies in a manger, wrapped in swaddling clothes.
Simeon: Did you hear? A Savior is born in Bethlehem!

Choir: "Angels We Have Heard on High"

Aaron: We must go and see this baby. We'll just walk across the hills and look all through the city until we find Him.
Simeon: In a manger, the angel said.
Aaron: Yes, lying in a manger.

Soloist: "What Child Is This?"

(Lights come on in the manger scene again.)

Singers: "While Shepherds Watched Their Flocks"

(Shepherds come in through the audience to the stage. They kneel at the manger. Joseph gives the baby to Mary again. As she holds Him, she sings "Away in a Manger.")

Mary: "Away in a Manger"

(Finale: All characters come on stage. JONATHAN speaks to FRANK.)

JONATHAN: You're right, Frank, this is the greatest Christmas I ever had. Now I know what Christmas is all about. What do you think, Mom?

MOM: I think it's wonderful! Thanks Frank, for helping us experience the true meaning of Christmas.

ALL: "Joy to the World!"

Curtain ☆

God's Special Lamb
Gwen Herder

Introduction: Baby Jesus was without a doubt the most remarkable gift ever given—the perfect Lamb of God sent to this earth to be a sacrifice for our sins. This program touches the hearts of both the participants and the audience as they marvel at Jesus, the Lamb of God. The program can easily be adapted for use with small to large Sunday schools, involving any number of children from ages 2 or 3 through sixth grade or above if desired.

All Scriptures are from the *New International Version* of the Bible.

Characters:
GRANDMA, GRANDPA, MOTHER, and FATHER—can be adults, youth or older children. *(Strong singing voices are helpful to sing along with children. MOTHER and FATHER are not assigned speaking parts, but could speak some of GRANDMA'S and GRANDPA'S.)*
NARRATOR
CHILDREN—grades 3 through 6 or adjusted to fit your situation. *(These children will sing together and have individual speaking parts—simply numbered 1, 2, 3, etc. to 40—to be assigned as your situation requires. For example, if you have 16 children participating, some can be assigned two lines and some three. All lines should be memorized.)*
MARY AND JOSEPH—adults, youth or children.
ANGELS—all girls in grades Kindergarten–2 *(or adjusted)*
SHEPHERDS—all boys in Kindergarten–2 *(or adjusted)*
LAMBS—all preschool children *(or adjusted)*

Scene 1—Grandma and Grandpa's home
Scene 2—Hillside outside Bethlehem
Scene 3—The manger
Scene 4—Grandma and Grandpa's home

Props: Scene 1 and Scene 4: two chairs; Bible; very few other items that can be removed quickly at the end of Scene 1 and set up again quickly for Scene 4. Wrapped Christmas gifts, including a lamb, and a tree can be set farther back and left on stage. The older children can carry in gifts as they enter. Scene 3—simple manger scene, easy to set up and take down; stool on which Mary can sit.

Sound and Lighting: For all scenes adequate microphones and speaker systems are needed. A lighting system that can be adjusted would be extremely helpful.

Costumes: All in Scenes 1 and 4 simply wear modern clothing. Mary, Joseph, and Shepherds wear appropriate biblical clothing, including shepherds' staffs. Angels need some angel costumes. Lambs need costumes that will identify them as lambs to help emphasize the program theme. *(Possibilities: 1. a lamb cap/face from fake fur; 2. on a white poster board, draw a lamb face and body, add black felt ears, cut holes for the face and arms.)*

Scene 1

GRANDMA and GRANDPA'S house; they are seated, GRANDPA is reading and GRANDMA is knitting. MOTHER and FATHER and modern CHILDREN enter from the main entrance. They come down one or more aisles, skipping joyfully and singing chorus and first verse of "Go, Tell It on the Mountain." All go up on stage, giving GRANDMA and GRANDPA hugs and greetings, placing their gifts under the tree and taking casual places. After all are in place, the first CHILD speaks.

1: I'm so excited. Christmas is wonderful.
2: So many presents. I can hardly wait to see what I got.
3: Coming to Grandma and Grandpa's house is the best part.
4: You can say that again. The food here is great! When do we eat?
GRANDMA: Hold on now. We'll eat soon enough, and there's plenty of food. But first we have a special gift to be opened. *(Picks up stuffed lamb gift.)* Here, ____, open it. It has a special meaning at Christmastime. *(Child 7 takes the gift, opens it while 5 and 6 speak.)*
5: Special gift, huh? I'll bet it's a video game.
6: No, I think it would be an MP3 player.
7 *(takes lamb, jumps up, gives GRANDMA and GRANDPA a hug):* Oh, Grandma, it's so cute. I just love it. What a precious little lamb. Thank you so much.
GRANDPA: We thought of you when we saw it. You always love the Bible stories about lambs.
8 *(taking lamb):* What's so special about a stuffed lamb?
GRANDMA *(taking lamb):* It's special because lambs are spoken of many times in the Bible. And Christmas is all about a very special Lamb. Does anyone know who that special Lamb is?

9: Since it's Christmas, it must be Jesus!

Grandpa: Indeed it is! Jesus is the most special Lamb of all. He is the Lamb of God!

10 *(taking lamb):* So a lamb really is a special Christmas gift after all—reminding us of Jesus.

Grandpa: Say, children, do you think we can let our imaginations work and pretend that we are out on a hillside close to Bethlehem on the night when Jesus was born? Let's join the shepherds and their sheep on that very special night.

Children: Sounds great! Let's go to Bethlehem. *(Give each other high fives.)*

Children (sing): "Jesus Is His Name" *(by Paul and Donna Williams; published in "Sing a Song of Scripture" 1984 by Lillenas Publishing Co.)*

(Children and adults on stage sing verses 1, 2, and 3. After song Scene 1 is quickly removed and older children and adults move to rear of stage while SHEPHERDS, ANGELS, and LAMBS enter. Music continues.)

Scene 2

On the hillside outside Bethlehem, ANGELS stand with backs to the audience. SHEPHERDS and LAMBS sit or lie, as if asleep.

Older Children: "Silent Night" *(Sing just the words, "Silent night, holy night, All is calm, all is bright" slowly, softly, then stop.)*

Narrator: "And there were shepherds living out in the fields nearby, keeping watch over their flocks at night" (Luke 2:8).

Older Children *(boldly sing):* "Glory to God in the Highest" *(by Joanne Barrett and Ron E. Long; published in "Sing a Song of Scripture," 1984 by Lillenas Publishing Co.)*

(While song is being sung, ANGELS turn and face the audience; SHEPHERDS and LAMBS stand. If desired, have younger children join older children in singing "Glory to God in the Highest" a second time.)

Angels: Shepherds, shepherds, do not fear. We have a message of love.
Shepherds, shepherds, do not fear. God sent His Son from above.
Shepherds, shepherds, go and see. See God's special Lamb.
Shepherds, shepherds, go and see. Born in Bethlehem.

Shepherds, shepherds, go and tell. Tell about God's Son.
Shepherds, shepherds, go and tell. Tell to everyone.

SHEPHERDS: Hurry shepherds, hurry! We must see this special one.
Hurry shepherds, hurry! We must worship God's own Son.
Hurry shepherds, hurry! We must go to Bethlehem.
Hurry shepherds, hurry! We must see God's special Lamb.
Hurry, hurry, hurry!

LITTLE LAMBS: Baa, baa, baa, baa, we want to go with you.
Baa, baa, baa, baa, we want to see Him, too.

SHEPHERDS: Yes, the little lambs can go. Jesus is God's Lamb you know.
Yes, the little lambs can go.

LITTLE LAMBS: Baa, baa, baa, baa, we will go with you.
Baa, baa, baa, baa, we will see Him, too.

ANGELS, SHEPHERDS, LAMBS *(sing):* "This Is the Way the Little Lambs Walk" *(Tune: "Here We Go Round the Mulberry Bush." Lambs or all do the actions.)*
This is the way the little lambs walk, *(walk in place)*
The little lambs walk, the little lambs walk.
This is the way the little lambs walk. We're going to see Jesus.
Verse 2—This is the way the little lambs hop. *(Hop.)*
Verse 3—This is the way the little lambs dance. *(Turn around.)*
Verse 4—This is the way the little lambs walk. *(Walk to manger.)*

(While children are singing, Scene 3 needs to be set up quickly on stage.)

Scene 3

The manger scene with MARY , JOSEPH, and manger in place. LAMBS, SHEPHERDS, and ANGELS gather round.

ANGELS, SHEPHERDS, LAMBS *(sing):* "Away in a Manger" *(2 verses with actions)*

ANGELS, SHEPHERDS, LAMBS *(sing):* "Jesus Is God's Special Lamb" *(Tune: "Mary Had a Little Lamb." Select your desired actions.)*
Jesus is God's special Lamb, special Lamb, special Lamb.
Jesus is God's special Lamb. Sent from Heaven above.
Jesus is God's special Lamb, special Lamb, special Lamb.
Jesus is God's special Lamb. Sent to show God's love.

LAMBS: We love You, baby Jesus.

MARY: Thank you for coming to see Jesus. He is God's special Lamb. And you are also special lambs of God. He loves every one.

ANGELS, SHEPHERDS, LAMBS *(sing):* "I Am Jesus' Little Lamb"*
I am Jesus' little lamb, happy all day long I am. *(Bounce arms up and down.)*
Jesus loves me, and I know that I'm His little lamb. *(Hug self, then bounce arms again.)*

(Pianist continues playing while LAMBS exit stage.)

ANGELS, SHEPHERDS: God sent His Son to be the Lamb,
To die upon the tree.
Jesus was that special lamb,
He died for you and me.

ANGELS, SHEPHERDS *(sing):* "Little Baby in the Manger" *(by Carrie B. Adams)*

(Pianist continues playing while ANGELS and SHEPHERDS exit. Scene 3 is removed and Scene 4 is set up quickly. Older children return to front stage.)

Scene 4

Everyone is back in GRANDMA and GRANDPA'S house.

11: That was fun, pretending we were right there on the hillside the night that Jesus the Lamb of God was born.
GRANDPA: Yes, it was fun! What else do you children remember about that very first Christmas?
12: An angel came to Mary and told her she would be the mother of God's own Son.
13: Imagine a real live angel taking to you. Wouldn't that be cool?
14: I know one thing that wasn't so good for Mary and Joseph. A mean old king made them travel to some far-off town right when Mary was ready to have a baby.
GRANDMA: Yes, things were very difficult back then. When the king commanded something, the people had better obey. Let's have Grandpa read us the story right from the Bible.
GRANDPA: I will read from Luke 2:1-7. *(Grandpa reads from the Bible.)*
15: They really had to go a long way.
16: And they didn't have any cars to go in then.
17: And no airplanes, either, to get there super fast.
18: They had to either ride a donkey or walk all the way.

19: Sure sounds hard to me. Walk for days and days! No way!
GRANDMA: It was hard, but God was with them all the way!
20: And after they finally made it to Bethlehem, they couldn't find any place to stay.
21: Poor Mary. She must have been so sad when the only place they could find in the whole town was a stable. And that's where Jesus was born.
GRANDPA: I believe God himself planned it that way. Just think. Jesus is the Lamb of God and He was born in a barn right in the middle of lambs, goats, cattle, and all.
22: When you think about it that way, a stable does seem like the perfect place for the Lamb of God to be born after all.

CHILDREN *(sing):* "The Stable"* *(by Floyd Robinson)*

23: We can't forget about the wise men coming.
24: And the gifts they brought—expensive gifts like gold and perfume.
25: I think the best part about the wise men was that God told them not to go back and tell the king where Jesus was.
26: The king had said he wanted to go and worship Jesus, but he was lying.
27: He was jealous. He didn't want to worship. He wanted to kill Jesus.
28: But an angel of God told Joseph to hurry and get Jesus out of town.
29: That must have been a scary night for poor Mary.
30: But God protected His special Lamb and kept Him safe from harm.

CHILDREN *(sing):* "Jesus Is His Name" *(music and chorus words by Paul and Donna Williams, published in "Sing a Song of Scripture" 1984 by Lillenas Publishing Co. Replace words to verses with the following words by Gwen Herder)*
Wise men journeyed to find the promised one. Jesus is His name.
A bright star led to God's holy Son. Jesus is His name.
(Chorus)
Wise men bowed and worshiped God's special Lamb. Jesus is His name.
Gave their gifts to the king, the great "I Am." Jesus is His name.
(Chorus.)

GRANDPA: Yes, Christmas reminds us of many things about Jesus the Lamb of God. Do you remember who called Jesus the Lamb of God?
31: I think it was John the Baptist just before Jesus was baptized.

Grandma: Right you are. Let's all repeat what John said.
All: "Look, the Lamb of God, who takes away the sin of the world!" (John 1:29).
32: How did Jesus take away the sin of the world?
Grandpa: Does any of you know what was the purpose of a lamb in the Old Testament?
33: A lamb was killed as a sacrifice for the sins of the people.
Grandma: And in the New Testament Jesus himself was the one who was killed as a sacrifice for our sins—Jesus was the Lamb of God who takes away the sin of the world.
Grandpa: Jesus could have just walked away when they tried to nail Him to the cross. But Jesus died on the cross because He loves us. He was God's special Lamb dying for you and me.
34: Jesus must have loved us a lot to die for us!
Grandma: He certainly did love us very much. That's what Christmas is really all about—the little baby who was the Lamb of God who died for us.

(Lights lowered during next two songs.)

Children: "The Child of Bethlehem"* *(Solo sung twice, then children join in singing, "The Lamb for sinners slain, bore the shame for all the world to see, The Child of Bethlehem died for me.")*

All: "Lamb of Glory" *(song by Greg Nelson and Phil McHugh)*

Grandpa: But the story of the Lamb of God does not end with Jesus' death.
35: I know. Three days later, He arose from the dead!
36: And He's alive today, isn't He?
Grandma: Indeed He is! And the very best news about the Lamb of God is still to come. Revelation, the last book in the Bible, tells us that Jesus the Lamb of God is sitting on a magnificent throne with people praising Him. Let's have Grandpa read it from the Bible.
Grandpa *(reads from Revelation 5:6, 11-14):* "Then I saw a Lamb, looking as if it had been slain, standing in the center of the throne. . . . I looked and heard the voice of many angels, numbering thousands upon thousands, and ten thousand times ten thousand. . . . In a loud voice they sang: 'Worthy is the Lamb, who was slain, to receive power and wealth and wisdom and strength and honor and glory and praise!' Then I heard every creature in heaven and on earth . . . singing:

'To Him who sits on the throne and to the Lamb be praise and honor and glory and power, for ever and ever!'"

37: Now that is quite a lamb story.

38: What a choir—thousands and thousands are singing praises to the Lamb.

39: I'll fit right in—praising Him in a loud voice.

40: Worthy is the Lamb who was slain.

ALL: "To the Lamb be praise and honor and glory and power, for ever and ever!" (Revelation 5:13).

CHILDREN *(sing):* "We Will Glorify" *(by Twila Paris, verses 1 and 4, published in "Sing a Song of Scripture," 1984 by Lillenas Publishing Co.)*

GRANDMA: Jesus, the Lamb of God came to a stable, went to the cross, rose triumphantly, and now is in Heaven with God the Father. What a magnificent ending it will be for the Lamb of God and for everyone who has accepted the Lamb who died to pay for their sins. I pray that all of you will accept Jesus as your Savior and that we'll all be together in Heaven worshiping the Lamb of God.

CHILDREN *(sing):* "O Come, Let Us Adore Him"

(Minister or someone may desire to offer an invitation and/or give closing remarks and prayer.)

* Some of these songs are from older, unknown sources. You may substitute with songs of your choosing. ☆

The True Meaning of Christmas

Cynthia Beadle

Children:

THREE SPEAKERS (two boys and one girl or two girls and one boy—all major parts listed as STEPHANIE, KERRIE, and BRANDON in the script)
MARY (doubles as woman at the tomb)
JOSEPH
INNKEEPER
LEAD ANGEL (girl—short speaking part)
ANGELS (girls)
LEAD SHEPHERD (to direct the other shepherds onto the stage)
SHEPHERDS (boys)
JESUS as a little boy (in the scene with the Wise men)
WISE MEN (three or four boys)
LADIES at tomb (girls)

Adults or Youth:

CHOIR
JESUS as an adult
ANGEL at the tomb

Props:

Notebook, pencil, two Bibles, biblical costumes, manger, doll, three gifts (for Wise men)

Scriptures are from the *International Children's Bible.*

KERRIE is standing center stage, a notebook in one hand, pencil in the other, writing something. STEPHANIE and BRANDON walk in, each with a Bible in the hand toward the audience.

STEPHANIE: Hi! What are you doing?
KERRIE: I'm making out my Christmas list.
BRANDON: The stuff you're going to give to your family?
KERRIE: No, what I'm going to get. I'm going to get everything I want this year and then some. My room will be better than a toy store. The kids in the neighborhood will have to come to my house to see

the latest in every kind of game or toy. And maybe I'll let them play with some of them, every once in a while.

STEPHANIE *(obviously not impressed):* That's nice.

(Short pause.)

KERRIE *(looking up from notebook):* So, what are you guys up to?

BRANDON: We're on our way to church to see the Christmas drama. You want to come with us?

KERRIE: No, thanks! I don't get into all that baby Jesus stuff. Besides, I have important work to do here.

(STEPHANIE and BRANDON look at each other.)

STEPHANIE: Well, you've missed the true meaning of Christmas.

KERRIE: I don't think so. My true meaning of Christmas is right here. *(Waves notebook)* Besides, when I get through celebrating the true meaning of Christmas, you two will be coming over to my house to play.

BRANDON: Getting lots of stuff for Christmas is nice, but I believe the true meaning of Christmas is the story of the baby born in Bethlehem. Have you ever heard the story?

KERRIE: Well *(looking a little embarrassed),* it has been a long time.

STEPHANIE: We've got the story right here. *(Opens Bible)* Let me read it to you.

KERRIE: If you insist!

STEPHANIE: "At that time, Augustus Caesar sent an order to all people in the countries that were under Roman rule. The order said that they must list their names in a register. This was the first registration taken while Quirinius was governor of Syria" (Luke 2:1, 2).

KERRIE: Who?

STEPHANIE: Quirinius.

BRANDON: He was appointed by the Roman Empire. They were in charge back then.

(Lights come up on stage. MARY and JOSEPH enter through the rear doors of the auditorium and come down the aisle as STEPHANIE continues to read. They go to the INNKEEPER, who shakes his head and waves his hands, turning them away. They go to the manger and sit down.)

STEPHANIE: *(Continues reading.)* "And everyone went to their own towns to be registered. So Joseph left Nazareth, a town in Galilee. He went to the town of Bethlehem in Judea. This town as known as the town of David. Joseph went there because he was from the family of David. Joseph registered with Mary because she was engaged to marry him. (Mary was now pregnant.) While Joseph and Mary were in Bethlehem, the time came for her to have the baby. She gave birth to her first son. There were no rooms left in the inn. So she wrapped the baby with cloths and laid him in a box where animals are fed" (Luke 2:3-7). *(Mary places doll in manger.)*

KERRIE: The baby was born in—uh—a feed box?

BRANDON: Well, they were in a barn. The city was so full of people coming in to be registered that they didn't have a place to stay.

(SHEPHERDS come in and are seated in front of the stage. LEAD ANGEL comes in quietly.)

KERRIE: Oh, I see. What happened next?

STEPHANIE: Well, let me see, where was I? *(Hesitates—giving SHEPHERDS time to take their places.)* "That night, some shepherds were in the fields nearby watching their sheep. *(Spotlight on LEAD ANGEL, who steps up to SHEPHERDS.)* An angel of the Lord stood before them. The glory of the Lord was shining around them, and suddenly they became very frightened" (Luke 2:8, 9).

LEAD ANGEL: "Don't be afraid, because I am bringing you some good news. It will be a joy to all the people. Today your Savior was born in David's town. He is Christ, the Lord. This is how you will know him: You will find a baby wrapped in cloths and lying in a feeding box" (Luke 2:10-12).

STEPHANIE: "Then a very large group of angels from heaven joined the first angel. All the angels were praising God, saying: 'Give glory to God in heaven, and on earth let there be peace to the people who please God'" (Luke 2:13, 14).

(CHOIR sings "Angels We Have Heard on High" while ANGELS enter and join LEAD ANGEL on stage. ANGELS can sing chorus with CHOIR. On the last verse, some ANGELS peek into the manger on their way out.)

STEPHANIE: "Then the angels left the shepherds and went back to heaven. The shepherds said to each other, 'Let us go to Bethlehem and see this thing that has happened. We will see this thing the Lord told us about.' So the shepherds went quickly and found Mary and Joseph. And the shepherds saw the baby lying in a feeding box. Then they told what the angels had said about this child. Everyone was amazed when they heard what the shepherds said to them. Mary hid theses things in her heart; she continued to think about them. Then the shepherds went back to their sheep, praising God and thanking him for everything that they had seen and heard. It was just as the angel had told them" (Luke 2:15-20).

(CHOIR sings "Go, Tell It on the Mountain" as the SHEPHERDS go up onto the stage, peek into the manger, jump for joy and exit. MARY, JOSEPH, baby and manger exit after the song.)

CHOIR: "Go, Tell It on the Mountain"

KERRIE: Is that the end of the story?
STEPHANIE: No, there's more. Some time later, wise men came from the eastern part of the world looking for baby Jesus. They stopped in Jerusalem to ask King Herod for directions, but Herod was jealous and wanted to kill Jesus. Let me read you this part. *(Continues reading.)* "The wise men heard the king and then left. They saw the same star they had seen in the east. It went before them until it stopped above the place where the child was. When the wise men saw the star, they were filled with joy. They went to the house where the child was and saw him with his mother, Mary. They bowed down and worshiped the child. They opened the gifts they brought for him. They gave him treasures of gold, frankincense, and myrrh. But God warned the wise men in a dream not to go back to Herod. So they went home to their own country by a different way" (Matthew 2:9-12).

(MARY, JOSEPH, and the CHILD JESUS come on stage. WISE MEN enter the rear doors of the auditorium and come down the aisle while CHOIR sings "We Three Kings." WISE MEN kneel before the CHILD, present their gifts, and leave. At the end of the song, MARY, JOSEPH, and JESUS leave.)

CHOIR: "We Three Kings"

KERRIE: That's a great story, but why is a little baby so important to Christmas? I mean, kings were born all the time back then. Why do we celebrate a holiday just because one baby was born?
BRANDON: It's not just His birth that makes Him different. It was His life and what He did for us. He grew up and when He was thirty years old, He began His public ministry. He preached sermons and taught people, healed the sick, made blind folks see and lame people walk, drove out demons from folks and did other miracles.

KERRIE: Cool! Sounds like a great guy.

BRANDON: He was not only a "great guy," He was the perfect Son of God. That's why God could use Him to save us from our sins.

KERRIE: Do what?

BRANDON: You see, Jesus was God's Son. He came down from Heaven and was born as a little baby so that He could experience life just as we do. He lived a normal life, but He never sinned. After He spent three years preaching, teaching, and doing miracles, the Pharisees and the people in Jerusalem wanted to kill Him.

KERRIE: Wanted to kill Jesus? How awful! First King Herod wanted to kill Him when He was a baby and now these people?

BRANDON: They really did kill Him. Let me read you that part. *(Stage is dark. ADULT JESUS enters from the rear and comes down the aisle with a spotlight following Him. Several boys prod and poke at him, and several girls follow behind. The boys "nail" him to a cross in the center of the stage.)* "They led Jesus to the place called Golgotha. (Golgotha means the Place of the Skull.) At Golgotha the soldiers tried to give Jesus wine to drink. This wine was mixed with myrrh. But He refused to drink it. The soldiers nailed Jesus to a cross. Then they divided his clothes among themselves. They threw lots to decide which clothes each soldier would get. It was nine o'clock in the morning when they nailed Jesus to the cross. . . . At noon the whole country became dark. This darkness lasted for three hours. At three o'clock Jesus cried in a loud voice, . . . 'My God, my God, why have you left me alone?'" (Mark 15:22-25, 33, 34).

KERRIE: Well, why did God leave Him alone?

STEPHANIE: Because Jesus had taken on himself all the sins of the world—your sins and mine and everyone else's—when He died. *(The lights go out completely, and JESUS exits.)* God can't look upon sin, so He turned away. But the best part is yet to come.

(The stage lights come back on. LADIES enter and come onto the stage.)

BRANDON: "The day after the Sabbath day was the first day of the week. At dawn on the first day, Mary Magdalene and another woman named Mary went to look at the tomb. At that time there was a strong earthquake. An angel of the Lord came down from heaven. The angel went to the tomb and rolled the stone away from the entrance. Then he sat on the stone" (Matthew 28:1, 2).

(Adult ANGEL enters and sits down.)

KERRIE: There sure were a lot of angels around back then.
STEPHANIE: Jesus' life was a really special time in history. The angels were there to remind the people to pay attention to Jesus.
BRANDON: And there's more.
ANGEL: "Don't be afraid. I know that you are looking for Jesus, the one who was killed on the cross. But he is not here. He has risen from death as he said he would. Come and see the place where his body was. And go quickly and tell his followers. Say to them: 'Jesus has risen from death. He is going into Galilee. He will be there before you. You will see him there. . . . Now I have told you" (Matthew 28:5-7).
BRANDON: *(reading)* "The women left the tomb quickly. They were afraid, but they were also very happy. They ran to tell Jesus' followers what had happened" (Matthew 28:8).

(LADIES and ANGEL leave.)

KERRIE: Wow! What a great ending to the story!!
BRANDON: Sure is! Jesus appeared to the disciples for 40 days after He was raised from the dead, and then He ascended into Heaven. And He sent the Holy Spirit, who helps us in our Christian lives each day.
STEPHANIE: Jesus wants you to accept Him as your Savior and live your life for Him. The Holy Spirit will help you live the kind of life that pleases Him.
KERRIE: You know, I want to know more about Jesus. I thik I will come to church with you. Now I see why all those toys I wanted aren't so important. Jesus is the true meaning of Christmas.

(All ACTORS, SPEAKERS, and CHOIR come back onto the stage and sing "Joy to the World!") ☆